KIDS THROUGHOUT HISTORY™

Kids During the American Civil War

Lisa A. Wroble

The Rosen Publishing Group's
PowerKids Press™
New York

Published in 1997 by The Rosen Publishing Group, Inc.
29 East 21st Street, New York, NY 10010

First Edition

Book Design: Danielle Primiceri

Photo Credits: Cover © Corbis-Bettmann; pp. 4, 7, 8, 16, 20 © Archive Photos; p. 11, 12, 15, 19 © Corbis-Bettmann.

Wroble, Lisa A.
    Kids during the American Civil War / Lisa A. Wroble.
        p.   cm.—(Kids throughout history)
    Includes index.
    Summary: Presents a child's perspective on the Civil War covering industrialization in the North, agriculture and slavery in the South, and daily life in both areas.
    ISBN 0-8239-5123-5
    1. United States—History—Civil War, 1861–1865—Children—Juvenile literature. [1. United States—History—Civil War, 1861–1865] I. Title. II. Series: Wroble, Lisa A. Kids throughout history.
E468.9.B76 1997
973.7'083—dc21   96-3585
                                                                                                          CIP
                                                                                                          AC

Manufactured in the United States of America

Contents

Civil War

A civil war is when groups of people in the same country fight each other. The American Civil War was between people in the northern states and people in the southern states. It lasted from April 1861 to April 1865.

Leaders from the North and South couldn't agree on how to run the United States. They argued over everything from public schools to **slavery** (SLAY-ver-ee). The southern states broke away and formed their own country, the **Confederacy** (kun-FED-er-uh-see). The northern states were called the **Union** (YOON-yun).

◄ *The American Civil War lasted for four years, longer than anyone expected.*

Life in the South

Many people in the South had huge farms called **plantations** (plan-TAY-shunz). They grew crops such as cotton, rice, and tobacco. Many plantation owners bought people shipped to the United States from Africa as slaves. Slavery meant that one person owned and controlled another person's life. Slaves were not paid for their work. They were property, "owned" by their masters. When they had children, those children became the property of their master.

Plantation owners needed the work of slaves to run such large farms and still make money.

The southern plantation owners relied on the slaves to work in the fields. ▶

Life in the North

People in the North did not agree with slavery. They were building **factories** (FAK-ter-eez) and using machines that worked faster than people could. The North wanted to stop slavery and build more factories. The South needed slavery to keep their farms going, so they pulled away from the North and formed the Confederacy. But President Abraham Lincoln, along with the North, wanted to keep the states **united** (yoo- NY-ted). President Lincoln thought this was worth fighting for, so he called for a war.

◀ *Once the war began, many women left home to work in factories that produced weapons.*

Divided Families

John lived on a farm in Kentucky. His family owned twelve slaves. Nat was a slave boy John's age. John and Nat were friends. They played together when Nat didn't have to work. When the war started, Kentucky was a "slave state" on the Union side. John's father joined the Union Army. He wanted to help keep the country together. Nat's brother joined the Union Army, too. He wanted to end slavery. But John's oldest brother joined the Confederate Army. He said that if the Union won, John's family would lose their slaves and their farm.

Many boys joined the army as drummers, beating out marching rhythms while the ▶ armies marched into battle.

Food

People thought the war would end quickly. But it didn't. Most of the fighting went on in the South. As it went on, more and more farms were destroyed. Food became hard to find. Most of the food grown on farms was taken by the army to feed the troops. Western Kentucky, where John lived, was in the middle of the fighting. When the Confederate and Union troops passed through, they took the food and **supplies** (suh-PLYZ) they needed. Only potatoes and bread were left. John and his family often went hungry.

◄ *The food that once fed the farmers now fed the Confederate and Union troops.*

Clothing

Just as the troops took food when they moved through John's town, they took blankets and clothing. John's mother had little cloth left to make any new clothes. Instead, she patched John's and Nat's **knickers** (NIK-erz). These were short pants that buttoned at the knee. They were held up by **suspenders** (sus-PEN-derz). John and Nat wore loose shirts, which were also patched. They went barefoot. John's mother wore long, full skirts with fitted jackets. Nat's mother and sisters wore the same types of clothes, but their skirts were less full.

Boys wore knickers and shirts, and girls wore long, full dresses. ▶

School

The North wanted free public schools for everyone, but the South did not. Before the war started, John went to a one-room schoolhouse every day. There he learned to read, write, and to add and subtract numbers. Most slave owners did not allow their slaves to learn to read and write. But John showed Nat what he learned at school. During the war, John did not go to school. With the men gone to fight in the war, John and Nat had to work hard on the farm.

◀ *Before the war, most boys and girls in the North went to public schools.*

Free Time

Life during the war was scary. John, Nat, and their families spent some days hiding in the cellar until the fighting in their area was over. When John and Nat were not working in the fields, they often went fishing. Sometimes they hunted rabbits or squirrels with slingshots. Any food they caught was eaten that night for dinner.

Young southern boys fished and hunted to help feed their families during the war. ▶

Letters Home

Soldiers wrote home to tell their families about the war. John, Nat, and their families waited to receive news. But the letters often took a long time to arrive. The letters told of the ugliness of battle and the homesickness of the soldiers. Although John's father and brother were on different sides, they both told of many hurt soldiers and not enough doctors or supplies. Nat's brother wrote that thousands of men and boys had been killed. He wrote that he missed his family.

◀ *People received news about the battles through letters from family members in the war.*

Changes

When the war ended, the North had won. The northern and southern states were united once again. Many changes had to be made. Slaves were set free. They had to find work and housing. Some moved to the North. Many buildings and farms in the South had been destroyed. Families that had once been wealthy were now poor. They needed to find work and housing, too. Through many years and a lot of hard work, President Lincoln's hope of a peaceful, united country would one day come true.

Glossary

Confederacy (kun-FED-er-uh-see) The group of eleven southern states that separated themselves from the United States.

factory (FAK-ter-ee) A building in which things are made using machines.

knickers (NIK-erz) Short, loose pants gathered at, or just above, the knee.

plantation (plan-TAY-shun) A large farm on which cotton, tobacco and sugar cane are grown.

slavery (SLAY-ver-ee) The system of one person "owning" another.

supplies (suh-PLYZ) The food and equipment that an army needs to live and fight.

suspenders (sus-PEN-derz) Straps worn over the shoulders to hold up pants.

Union (YOON-yun) The United States; the northern states during the American Civil War.

united (yoo-NY-ted) Bringing someone or something together.

Index